THE WARRIOR PRINCESS 2

: SIKH WOMEN IN BATTLE

*The moving story of Guru Gobind Singh
through the eyes of four
saintly Sikh warrior women.*

Written by Harjit Singh

Illustrated by Harjit Singh "Artist"

Cover design by Taranjit Singh

ISBN 1-903863-01-5

Published by www.Sikh-Heroes.com
Email: harjit@sikh-heroes.com

Printed and Bound in India by
B. Chattar Singh Jiwan Singh (Exports)
Bazar Mai Sewan, Amritsar (India)
Tele : 0183-2542346, 2547974
Fax : 0183-2557973
E-Mail : csjs@jla.vsnl.net.in

DEDICATION

To my daughters HarSimran and
Tavleen Kaur ... be inspired!

CONTENTS

The founder of Sikhism, Guru Nanak Dev lived and preached that women were equal to men in the eyes of God. He wrote :

"From woman,
man is born;
within woman,
man is conceived;
to woman he is engaged
and married.

Woman becomes his friend;
through woman,
the future generations come.
When his woman dies,
he seeks another woman;
to woman he is bound.

So why call her bad?"

Guru Granth Sahib, 473

BACKGROUND

For thousands of years, India faced attacks from foreign invaders. As they entered, they wiped their feet on the North-western state of Punjab and faced little resistance. Some came for gold and women, but in 1526 the powerful Mughal Empire came for more, much more. They came to conquer.

A terrible shadow fell over the land. Some of the Emperors were butchers and filled the uneducated and superstitious villagers with fear. But, the dark night began to clear with rising sun. God sent Guru Nanak Dev, the first Sikh Guru, to bring a new dawn into the world. His message was of peace, love and service to humanity. The fifth Guru, Guru Arjun Dev, was a beautiful flower, spreading God's fragrance to one and all. His teachings reached out to the rich and poor, to men and women, to Hindus and Muslims.

The Mughal Emperor Jehangir was furious that Sikhism was flourishing. In 1606, he ordered the slow torture of the fifth Guru over five long days and nights to force him to convert to Islam. The Guru smiled and accepted death saying, "God's will is sweet."

When all peaceful means have been exhausted it is right to use the sword. The next Guru was the first Sikh warrior. Guru HarGobind fought four successful defensive battles and established Sikh independence. Peace followed for a while.

History repeated itself in 1675 when the Mughal Emperor Aurangzeb beheaded Guru Tegh Bahadur - the ninth Sikh Guru. Aurangzeb thought of himself as a good Sunni Muslim, but in reality he was a fanatic. He was ruthless and only became Emperor by overthrowing his father and killing his three brothers. He banned music and poetry. He ordered Hindu and Sikh temples to be destroyed. Non-Muslims were banned from working for him and forced to pay double the tax. He even persecuted Muslims with different beliefs from his own - the Shias and the Sufis. He was so arrogant that he declared himself to be the ruler of the world.

He gave non-Muslims two choices : Islam or death. The Hindu leaders begged the prophet of peace, the ninth Guru to help them. He immediately took his three closest Sikhs and headed to Delhi to protest. The Emperor arrested them and gave them the choice : Islam or death. After torturing the three Sikhs, the Guru was beheaded. He left a note, "I gave my head, but not my principles. I gave my head, but not my faith."

Now another Gobind meaning protector of the world, carried on the mission. Guru Gobind Singh saw that all peaceful means had been exhausted. Once again it was time to unsheathe the sword. In 1699 he created the Khalsa - The Army of God. Infront of tens of thousands he initiated the beloved five volunteers with *amrit*, the holy water. Then to everyone's surprise and he performed the greatest act of humility. The Guru kneeled infront of the five and was initiated too. This *amrit* ceremony gave the followers complete spiritual and physical rejuvenation.

Thousands and thousands were initiated into the Khalsa. Day after day, men and women, high and low castes, rich and poor began a new life. Theses fearful sparrows became mighty hawks. Jackals turned into lions with the courage to face a whole army single handed.

But the enemy was not Islam, it was the oppressor who misused it. Guru Gobind Singh wrote, "The temple and the mosque are the same. The Hindu and the Muslim ways of worship lead to the same end. Recognise the human race as one."

The Guru along with his Khalsa fought many battles against small time corrupt Hindu warlords and bringing law and order to the land.

Seeing the growing power of the Guru and the Khalsa, Emperor Aurangzeb and the Hindu warlords decided to destroy the Guru once and for all. Hundreds of thousands of their combined armies surrounded the Guru and his Khalsa. They sieged the fort of Anandgarh from May 1705 for over six months. That is where the stories in this book begin.

INTRODUCTION

Welcome to the second book in the Warrior Princess series. These true stories are brought to life through the eyes of Sikh women. They will take you through one of the saddest times in Sikh history. In December 1705, Guru Gobind Singh was betrayed by the Emperor along with a former cook and worst of all by forty of his own Sikhs.

The first story is called "The Siege" and shows how Guru Gobind Singh, his family and his Sikhs were trapped inside the Anandgarh Fort by the Hindu-Muslim Combined Forces. Forty of the Sikhs deserted. Their story is completed in "The Fearless Leader" when Mai Bhago, a brave young woman changed their destiny.

The rest of the Sikhs left with Guru Gobind Singh were attacked and separated. The tragic story of the Guru's mother and his younger sons is told in "The Grandmother". The heroic story of the older sons is told in "The Cremation".

THE
SIEGE

The raging Mughal troops screamed the battle cry, "GOD IS GREAT!!!!!" One hand on their horse reigns and the other wielding a mighty sword. They charged up the hill determined to smash the fortress gates this time. A thousand arrows rained down. It was useless, they could not penetrate Anandgarh, the Khalsa fort.

"RETREAT! RETREAT!" screamed a desperate Governor Wazir Khan as he watched hundreds of his soldiers crash to the ground.

Back at base camp, the Generals were summoned for an emergency meeting. The jungle nights were cold, and hundreds of camp fires were seen all around the base of the hill. Anandgarh Fort stood on top, impenetrable and untouched.

"Six MONTHS Jabardast Khan. Six long, hard months in this wretched, mosquito infested jungle. When are those fortress rats going to give up?"

"Be patient General, even rats die one day."

"Patient! How much more patient can we be? We massively outnumber Gobind Singh's army. Yet they have killed thousands of our soldiers and we've barely scratched the fortress walls."

A couple of guards stood at the entrance. The wind howled, the tent shook and sent the lanterns swinging above the seated officers. At the head, a larger, more impressively dressed man stood up. The Governor Of Sirhind, Wazir Khan raised his palm and signalled for calm.

"Sit down Generals. His excellency Emperor Aurangzeb has placed me in charge. We must review our tactics. We have the Hindu warlords with us, we have the victorious army of Jabardast Khan with us, and we have the military might of the Mughal Empire. Fellow Generals, we have under estimated these Khalsa rats. Even though their army is small, we have not been able to beat them through our siege. They have the superior position on the hilltop. Think of another plan Generals."

"I still believe patience is the best strategy Governor. It has been several months since we imposed the siege. I believe our siege is working. We have cut off all supplies of food to the fort; those rats must be almost starved by now. If we just wait another few months, victory will be ours..."

"How can you say that Jabardast Khan! Another few months means spending a cold and miserable winter here. Our camp hospitals are already bursting at the seams with sick soldiers. Those wretched floods last month brought so much disease. Hundreds of soldiers are dying every day. There is low morale amongst the troops and thousands of soldiers are deserting us every week. Do any of us want to spend the rest of winter like this?

NO! WE MUST LURE OUT THE KHALSA RATS AND FINISH THEM WITH OUR SWORDS!"

At hearing Governor Wazir Khan, the Generals cheered and drove their swords into the air.

* * *

"What do you think of the letter from Aurangzeb?" asked Mata Gujri, "He's promised on the Koran that no harm will come to us if we leave now. Many of the Khalsa soldiers have asked me to request you take up the offer. Their morale is low and they are down to eating leaves and tree bark."

"Mother, it's nothing but a trick. Why would Aurangzeb let us go safely when he's been trying to kill us for months? Remember this is the same Emperor who grabbed the throne by killing his brothers and imprisoning his father. No one should leave the fort yet. I'll show you the value of his word."

But, unable to stand any further starvation, forty of the Guru's Khalsa soldiers signed a letter of resignation declaring that they were no longer Sikhs of the Guru. They turned their backs in shame and packed their meagre belongings. The remaining Sikhs were desperate too, but would not leave the Guru's side.

That night the Guru sent out a few mules carrying old sacks and fire torches on their horns. It

looked like the Sikhs had packed and were taking up the offer of safe passage. Mughal soldiers came charging towards the fort and ripped open the sacks looking for treasures. They found old shoes and rags instead. In the confusion the forty deserters managed to escape through enemy lines.

The next day a messenger arrived offering a silver tray on his outstretched palms.

There was a letter and two holy books : the Muslim General's Koran and the Hindu warlord's Gita. They apologised for the attack last night and said it was the work of a few dishonest soldiers who had now been punished. They promised on their holy books that they would not attack if the Guru left.

Unconvinced, Guru Gobind Singh decided to stay at the fort.

"You are our Guru, we live and die for you," said a devoted Sikh, "but we have lost so many warriors and have been out of food for weeks. You are our king in this world and the next. It makes no difference to us if we live at your feet in this world or the next, but this world needs you. You must survive, if you stay here you will starve to death with the rest of us."

"My beloved Khalsa, it is more noble to die fighting than to starve to death. I will go with the leading group and test Aurangzeb's promise. If we safely pass then the remaining group of women warriors led by Dalair Kaur will follow."

"Your words are true my Guru," replied Dalair Kaur, "bless us so we may do this duty with honour."

Guru Gobind Singh tapped Dalair Kaur's shoulder with the golden tip of his arrow.

* * *

At midnight on the 5th December, 1705, Guru Gobind Singh's group left the fort. The combined Hindu and Mughal forces quickly abandoned their promises. They charged after Guru Gobind Singh and his band of 1500 Khalsa. Some of the Combined Forces rode to the fort, burning and looting everything in their way.

Guru Gobind Singh later wrote of this treachery to Emperor Aurangzeb :

I did not know that you
were a breaker of promises,
a lover of wealth
and lacking true faith in God.
You are not solid in your Islamic beliefs,
you do not have the real knowledge of God,
nor do you have any faith in your prophet.
A truly religious person
would never swerve from his promise.

Guru Gobind Singh, ZafarNama

Dalair Kaur saw that her beloved Guru and Khalsa had been betrayed. She prepared everyone for battle, "Sisters, we have given our heads to our Guru at the amrit initiation ceremony. We have lived for Truth, now the time has come to die for it. Sisters remember that we are all trained warriors and we will die fighting rather than living like slaves. Pick up your weapons and get in position and remember that GOD IS TRUE!"

The enemy soldiers thought that the fort was empty and were taken aback by the sudden rain of arrows and bullets. Within a few minutes, hundreds of dead soldiers lay outside the fort. Seeing this, the remaining soldiers left their positions and ran for their lives. Governor Wazir Khan was furious at not having captured the fort. He started screaming at his men, "FIRE THE CANNON! FIRE THE CANNON."

Intense cannon fire succeeded in breaking through a wall of the fort. The ground troops charged into another storm of bullets. The ruthless Wazir Khan sent more and more troops. Eventually the Khalsa ran out of ammunition. Governor Wazir Khan smiled as capture was imminent.

Dalair Kaur gathered her sisters-in-arms together one last time, "We have fought well, now our time has come to die. It is up to us to die with honour. Sisters, remember the brave women from Rajput. When their husbands had died in battle and their fort was about to be captured, they would all jump into a fire and burn to death rather than let the enemy dishonour them. This was how their religion taught them to preserve

23

their honour. Our Guru is always with us. He protects our honour. Sisters, our Guru has trained us as warriors and we will die fighting along side our husbands and brothers. Remember we are lionesses."

The enemy was advancing so rapidly that there was no time for further speeches. Dalair Kaur gave the signal and all the Khalsa warriors drew their swords and positioned themselves behind the damaged wall. This was the only way for the enemy to enter.

Mighty soldiers began climbing in over the piles of rubble. When they saw so many Khalsa women ready for battle they stopped in their tracks. They were expecting to find hundreds of Khalsa men, they never knew women could be warriors.

Witnessing the events from a distance, Governor Wazir Khan yelled, "Cowards, are you afraid of women? They are gifts for you, capture them and do what you want with the rewards of your hunt."

Dalair Kaur yelled back, "We are the hunters, not the hunted. Come forward and find out for yourself!"

Governor Wazir Khan took up the challenge and sent his men forward. Khalsa lionesses attacked them from every corner. Not knowing how many other Khalsa warriors were in the fort the Mughals retreated yet again. Governor Wazir Khan started yelling at his men, "FIRE THE CANNON! FIRE THE CANNON."

Powerful cannon fire destroyed the already weakened wall. The fort's inner compound was clearly visible and no Khalsa warriors could be seen. The Governor was convinced that no one was left alive and this time he took thousands of troops with him into the fort. They searched every inch of the fort but did not find anyone. The Governor was furious. Where did the Khalsa lionesses disappear too? He screamed at his men to find them.

The soldiers searched cautiously, expecting a surprise attack from any direction. Finally, they concluded that the remaining Khalsa warriors must have escaped through some secret passage.

Orders were given to abandon the search and to start looting. The very soldiers who were afraid for their lives started searching for wealth inside the fort. When they removed the piles of rubble from the fallen wall they found no buried treasure; they only found the bodies of Dalair Kaur and the women martyrs of Anandgarh Fort.

ZAFARNAMA :
THE LETTER OF VICTORY

Guru Gobind Singh wrote this victory letter to
Aurangzeb after being tricked out of the fort with
tragic results.   Here are some extracts :

Those who had relied
on your oath on the Koran
should not have been
arrested or killed.

A man should be true to his words.
He should not think in one way
and act in another.

Recognise God -
do not break anyone's heart
or injure their feelings
without reason.

If you carelessly use the sword
to suck people's blood,
God will shed your blood
in the same way.

*Anandgarh Fort still stands at the top of the hill.
Anandpur Sahib, Punjab.*

28

Gurdwara Parwar Vichora stands by the river exac...,
where the Guru's family were separated. Sirsa, Punjab.

29

THE
CREMATION

The icy wind howled through the trees around the village. Nothing but darkness and a few sleeping cows surrounded the lonely houses. A small lamp burned inside Bibi Sharan Kaur's house.

She had just finished her bedtime prayer and was pulling back the layers of thick blankets from her wooden bed. She was tired of the persecution of Guru Gobind Singh and her beloved Khalsa.

It had been a long day, she had been up since two in the morning to meditate. She had milked the cows in the darkness, and gathered fire wood before the rest of the village woke up. Widowed at a young age and now in her fifties, she spent her life living alone, meditating on God.

Sitting on the bed she reached over to the bed-side table and picked up her sandalwood beads. They brought a smile to her face.

She remembered how over a decade earlier she used to look after the older sons of the Guru.

33

Ajit Singh and Jujhar Singh were as brave as their names : invincible warriors. They would always be trying to get her to sword fight with them. But she was happier meditating by saying "Waheguru" as she pressed each bead with her forefinger and thumb. She would tell them she was praying for them, that they were handsome princes whom the whole world would remember.

Since her husband had died fighting the Mughals, she had devoted her life to taking care of the Guru's older sons. In fact, they were the sons she never had. She had spent her happiest days with their smiling faces. But times had changed, they had grown up into handsome teenagers and she had not seen them for over a year. She had heard they had been trapped for the last six months inside the fort of Anandgarh – sieged by Mughal forces.

Everyday she prayed for their well being. They meant more to her than her own life – she would do anything for them. Anything.

"Bibi Sharan Kaur! Bibi Sharan Kaur!"

She heard someone whispering outside her door.

"Who's there?" she asked as she cautiously approached the door.

"Bibi Sharan Kaur have you forgotten me already?"

Her heart leapt, she rushed forward and unbolted the door.

A handsome warrior stood infront of her. He had a radiant face, beautiful black beard and tall turban. Bibi Sharan Kaur fell immediately to his holy feet.

"What a wonderful day – Guru Gobind Singh, wonderful Guru, Waheguru! Waheguru! I am so blessed to have you sacred vision."

Guru Gobind Singh helped Bibi Sharan Kaur up. As she rose she saw his clothes were torn and muddy. He had lost a lot of weight and his forearms and calves were full of small cuts and scratches. But to those who had spiritual eyes, his face and body glowed like a thousand blazing suns.

Behind the Guru she saw the shadows of two more warrior Singhs approaching.

"Have you brought your sons with you. Is that Ajit Singh and Jujhar Singh? Will I be blessed to see the smiling faces of my handsome princes?"

As the lamplight lit their faces, Bibi Sharan Kaur realised it was Daya Singh and Dharam Singh. Behind them came Maan Singh – he was the last one in and cautiously looked back over the village to make sure no one had followed them. He quietly closed the door.

They all looked very rough and dirty. Their uniforms were in shreds and all kinds of axes, swords, and punch-daggers were strapped across their backs and waists.

Bibi Sharan Kaur served them food and water and provided clean blankets and clothes. After a little rest, the blessed guests were ready to leave.

Maan Singh spoke, "These are terrible times and

your service is greatly appreciated. But we have to leave now while it is still dark."

The warrior saints stood up.

"Please stay for a day or two – it has been so long. I have so much to ask all of you."

"If we stay your life will be in danger. We are being pursued by Mughals and they will destroy the whole village if they find us here."

"Before you go you must tell me what happened – where are my handsome princes?"

"Bibi Sharan Kaur, over five hundred of us left the fort three days ago, but we were tricked. The Mughals attacked us after they had promised to let us go freely. As we approached the Sirsa river we saw it was flooded. Many Khalsa brothers drowned helping the women to get across. Lots of the Guru's writings were destroyed too."

"Was Ajit Singh one of those who drowned?"

"No, Ajit Singh was a hero because he delayed

the Mughals. He bravely took lead of a group of Singhs. They fought the Mughals while the rest of us crossed the furiously raging river. Finally, he crossed as well and left the Mughals standing scared on the bank; waiting for him to drown. When his soaked horse stepped onto our side, the Mughals pulled their horses back and waved their swords in frustration.

"Those poor Singhs who drowned - their mothers should be proud their sons died helping others survive."

"They were closer to me than my own family. I wanted to get their bodies to cremate them, but we were suddenly attacked by a local tribe. We lost many more Singhs. We had to separate - it was the safest option, and in the confusion we had no other choice."

"What happened to the Guru's mother?"

"Mata Gujri and the younger princes, Zorawar Singh and Fateh Singh escaped into the jungle. The Guru's wife Mata Sundri and the Mother of the Khalsa, Mata Sahib Kaur headed for Delhi.

We told the majority of the Khalsa to meet us in a few days. The remaining forty of us went with the Guru to the town of Chamkaur. We hid in an old mud fortress at the top of a hill."

"I know something terrible happened. That is why you still haven't told me about my princes, Ajit Singh and Jujhar Singh."

Maan Singh placed his hand on Bibi Sharan Kaur's shoulder and sat down next to her.

"Terrible things did happen. We were surrounded on all sides by the Mughals. We were prepared to die."

Guru Gobind Singh spoke, "What could forty hungry men do when suddenly attacked by one million invaders? Those breakers of promises came with great speed and started firing. Having been attacked and with no other choice, we had to jump into battle and use arrows and gunfire in defence. When all peaceful methods fail it is right to draw the sword."

Maan Singh continued, "We decided to split up

into groups of five. We planned that each group would go out and fight. When they died then the next group would go. It was the only way to hold the Mughals off. All of a sudden we heard them charging uphill towards our outer mud wall."

Guru Gobind Singh added more detail, "The Mughal soldiers, clad in black uniforms came like swarms of flies and started shouting. I fired arrows over the wall and killed them instantly. No one else came forward after that."

Maan Singh took a sip of water and put his cup down. "After a short time the Mughals resumed their attacks and we started sending out groups of five brave Khalsa. They fought like true heroes."

"When I saw Nahar Khan in the battlefield," said the Guru, "I immediately gave him a taste of my arrow. The arrogant soldiers with him fled. Then one notable soldier entered the battle with the speed of a bullet. He led many attacks, some intelligently and others foolishly."

Maan Singh turned to Bibi Sharan Kaur, "Ajit Singh came forward and requested his Guru-father to allow him to go and die with honour. He fought like a true hero. On seeing him die, his younger brother Jujhar Singh valiantly came forward. He too died a noble death. The soldier with the speed of a bullet led both the attacks that killed them."

Guru Gobind Singh stood up, "That soldier received many wounds, and after killing my sons he himself lay dead!"

Bibi Sharan Kaur could not control her tears, she said, "They were only 18 and 16 years old. They had their whole life ahead of them. What kind of people are the Mughals – have they no mercy?"

"The Mughal leaders are cowards," said Maan Singh. "They brought one million soldiers to fight forty of us. Even their Commander refused to come onto the battlefield."

The Guru spoke, "That cursed Mughal Commander did not come out from behind his wall all night. If I had seen his face, I would have fired an arrow and put him into eternal sleep."

"The Mughals are fanatics and we have to stand together to destroy them," said Maan Singh. "That is why when Guru Gobind Singh told us he was going out to single handedly destroy as many Mughals as possible, we stopped him. The Guru wouldn't listen to us, but we gathered as five, the Guru Khalsa, and made the decision that the survival of the Guru was more important than anything else."

The Guru added, "In the end, with arrows and guns firing, brave soldiers died on both sides. There was so much bloodshed that the ground looked like a field of red poppy flowers. Heads and feet were heaped up everywhere - they looked like balls on a playground. Soldiers were screaming from arrows and gunshot wounds. The arrows had caused so much havoc that even the strongest soldiers lost their senses. What could forty brave Khalsa do when swarms of the enemy pounced on them?"

Bibi Sharan Kaur wiped away her tears and asked, "So how did you escape?"

"We were down to the last group of five Khalsa.

Sant Singh and Sangat Singh remained at the mud fort to create the impression we still had a strong army. Then in the darkness of night the three of us and the Guru sneaked out through gaps in the Mughals encirclement. We have crawled over forest floors and we have eaten nothing, but we will do anything for Guru Gobind Singh."

Bibi Sharan Kaur turned to the Guru, she knelt at his holy feet and placing her hands together she made a request.

"My Guru, you are the true King in this world and the next. My Guru, grant me one wish. Without my young princes on this earth, I have no desire to stay here. Let my soul go to the next world."

Guru Gobind Singh consoled Bibi Sharan Kaur and told her it was more noble to die for a cause. After that they left to complete their great escape.

Bibi Sharan Kaur's heart ached, something had died inside her. She wanted to die, but the Guru's words kept ringing in her ears '... may I die for a cause ...'

She was not a trained warrior, but she headed towards the town of Chamkaur. She had decided to find the bodies of the martyred Khalsa soldiers and her handsome princes and give them a proper cremation. Just the thought of them rotting amongst Mughal corpses on a blood drenched battlefield horrified her. She knew the Mughal soldiers would be like vultures looking for their bodies so they could claim a reward.

Bibi Sharan Kaur reached the battlefield in the early hours – there was death and destruction everywhere. The last two Singhs at the mud fortress had been killed and there was no trace of the Mughal army – they must have moved on.

She stepped through the battlefield and repectfully dragged the bodies of the Khalsa warriors together. When she found the young princes, she wiped their faces with a wet cloth and kissed their foreheads. She prayed for them and brought fire wood from the forest and the makeshift fortress. She built a funeral pyre around all of the bodies and lit it with the flame in her oil lamp.

She sat down nearby and stared into the rising flames. She read the final prayer, Sohila, and brought peace to the warzone. As the fire raged higher and brighter, she closed her eyes and turned the beads between her fingers. "Waheguru Waheguru Waheguru Waheguru" churned her spirit. Feeling the love of the Immortal God her spirit rose up out through the top of her head, the dasam duar. She entered deep meditation, samadhi , and became completely unaware of her body and surroundings. Like a drop of water merging into the ocean, like the flames of the fire reaching for the Sun, she was completely absorbed in the love of the Lord.

The now raging fire had attracted a band of Mughal soldiers. Seeing a middle aged woman sitting at the edge they surrounded her. Someone shouted at her.

"Who are you?"

Bibi Sharan Kaur didn't move a muscle.

"What are you doing?"

Bibi Sharan Kaur sat frozen like a rock.

The soldiers lost patience and realising she was a Sikh prodded her with the tips of their spears and swords.

Even as her clothes ripped and blood seeped through, Bibi Sharan Kaur's spirit remained with Waheguru.

Unable to understand how this old woman could sit and take the pain of sword tips and spears, they pushed her over. Throwing insults and kicking her like a football, they started slashing her body.

There was still no sound or movement from Bibi Sharan Kaur.

The Mughals felt the heat from the fire and turned around. They saw the faces of Ajit Singh and Jujhar Singh about to turn to ashes and grabbed hold of Bibi Sharan Kaur's upper arms. Shaking her one shouted, "We would have got a huge reward for taking their heads. But you just burnt it all away."

Once again there was no reply from Bibi Sharan Kaur. The Mughals were furious and started pushing Bibi Sharan Kaur. She did not fight back.

The Mughals tried to stamp the fire out and started kicking the outer pieces of wood, but the brave lioness had completed her mission. Frustrated by Bibi Sharan Kaur's silence they grabbed her arms and legs and tossed her into the fire shouting "You love them so much you can die with them!"

Bibi Sharan Kaur protected the honour of Ajit Singh and Jujhar Singh and the Guru's brave Khalsa. Waheguru granted her desire to leave her body after dying for a cause.

As the flames engulfed her, her body perished but her spirit was forever drenched in the love of the Lord.

FATEHNAMA :
THE LETTER OF VICTORY

These extracts are from the first letter of victory
to Emperor Aurangzeb:

I will place fire under your feet

and will not allow you

to drink the water of Punjab.

Using deception, so what

if the sly fox has killed

two cubs of a lion?

The lion is still alive

and sure to get justice.

Now I do not ask you for anything

in the name of your Allah and Koran.

*Gurdwara KathalGarh Sahib : the place where
Baba Ajit Singh and Baba Jujhar Singh fought,
died and were cremated. Chamkaur Sahib, Punjab.*

THE GRAND-MOTHER

"Step this way Mata Gujri," Gangu Brahmin looked back at the eighty-five year old woman and her two young grandsons walking alongside the donkey. He jerked the reigns forward, "FASTER YOU STUPID DONKEY!"

The sounds of the Mughals horses and the crashing river had long faded into the distance. They were replaced by thousands of crickets clicking louder and louder in the night air. After Mata Gujri and her grandsons had been separated from the Guru at the river battle, they ended up in a nearby town called Ropar. There they met Gangu a former servant of the Guru. He was so happy to see them that he offered to take them home.

"Gangu are you sure this is the right way?"

"O Mata Gujri I played in these forests as a child. I have cooked for the rich using the finest wild herbs in this forest. Of course I know the way to my own village. I know its been a while since I stopped working for the Guru, but surely you still trust me?"

"Of course I trust you Gangu and I am very grateful that you brought your donkey to carry our bags. Now forget I said anything and just get us to your house. I need to get the children out of their dirty clothes from the terrible river crossing."

Gangu walked ahead and started mumbling to himself, "I was the best cook Guru Gobind Singh had. There is no one as good as me in this whole country and look at me now - risking my life to save the Guru's sons and mother. There is no one as good as me so the Guru better give me a gold coin for rescuing his family. On second thoughts he should give me a handful of gold coins - it is his mother and children after all!"

Mata Gujri ignored Gangu's mumbling and carefully stepped through the undergrowth. She grabbed the six year old Fateh Singh's arm, "Be careful my child, there is a snake curled up by that tree."

The eight year old Zorawar Singh drew his sword, "I will slice its head off in one swift swing Grandma!"

"No, no, my child only use your sword for self-defence. The snake means us no harm. Just be careful not to disturb it."

Zorawar Singh grabbed Fateh Singh's hand, "Don't worry Grandma, I will look after my brother." Fateh Singh looked up, "Grandma, will we ever see our mother, father and brothers again?"

"Don't worry little one, everything is in Wahegu-ru's hands. We'll have a good nights rest and find out where they are in the morning."

They entered Gangu's village to the sounds of howling wolves in the distance. A thick veil of darkness surrounded them. Fateh Singh looked down and could not even see where his feet were stepping, "Zorawar Singh I don't like this village; it's really creepy."

Zorawar Singh put his arm around his little broth-er's shoulders and hugged him close, "I'll always be by your side brother."

Gangu lead them along the dirt tracks. They went around the muddy puddles and could see the outlines of sleeping cows lying infront of some of the tiny mud houses.

"Here we are Mata Gujri."

Gangu tied up the donkey and unloaded the saddle bags. Stepping through the front door he lit the lamp.

"I hope you don't mind that my house is very small. I'm only a poor Hindu cook, but everything I have is yours so make yourself at home."

Mata Gujri looked around at the crumbling bricks and mud plastered ceiling. Twigs, branches and dry mud had been bundled together to keep out the rain. Mata Gujri was used to such things and replied slowly and wisely, "Gangu my son, when we die, God the Divine Judge, will ask us what we did in our lives. God will not ask us how much money we had or how big our house was. Gangu while you love us , your house is a palace for us."

Gangu pressed both palms together and humbly tilted his head forward, "You are too kind Mata

Gujri. Now let me show you to your room." He picked up Mata Gujri's bags and led the way.

Mata Gujri got the young princes ready. She recited the evening prayer and meditated on Waheguru. Lying down in the middle of the bed, the princes used her arms as pillows.

"Grandma sing to us," requested Fateh Singh.

Mata Gujri closed her eyes and hugged the boys closer. The sweetest voice you every heard sang a verse from the holy scriptures.

The young princes fell asleep thinking of God.

There was a quiet knock on the door and Gangu entered, "Here's a jug of water for you Mata Gujri in case you get thirsty."

"Just leave it on the table next to my bag."

Gangu noticed a gold coin in the bag as he put the jug down, "In the morning Mata Gujri, I will find out where the Guru and his sons are."

"Gangu, my son, you are a good man. I have been praying for them since we were betrayed by the Mughals when we left the fort. I think I would die if anything happened to any of my grandsons."

"Yes, we are living in difficult times Mata Gujri. It is hard to know who we can trust nowadays."

Gangu left the room and Mata Gujri looked at the sleeping princes. A tear came to her eye as she thought of all the suffering they had endured. Firstly, the seven months of being slowly starved in the siege at Anandgarh Fort. Then being chased by the Mughals across the river and seeing so many Sikhs drown. Then being parted from their mother and Guru-father in all the confusion. And now having to march through the dark forest in wet clothes.

She wiped away her tears and kissed them on the forehead. She caressed their radiant faces with her wrinkled hands and whispered "Sleep well my precious jewels, sleep well."

She blew out the candle and fell asleep for a

couple of hours. That was all she needed. She did not eat much either. Her hunger was not for worldly possessions, but for God's name. Arising well before sunrise, Mata Gujri bathed and sat comfortably in meditation. Waheguru had been pleased with her devotion from a tender age. She had been blessed with the knowledge of God.

Mata Gujri had served her husband, Guru Tegh Bahadur, while he meditated in the underground room for twenty-six and half years. God was preparing him for the greatest self-sacrifice in history. Through her humble devoted service to her Guru-husband she was blessed with the perfect son, Guru Gobind Singh. The one sent by God to destroy the tyrants and to protect the saints.

Mata Gujri closed her eyes and her spirit went to the highest realm of Truth. It merged with the Supreme and enjoyed God's love light, the unstruck melody and divine bliss. All worldly thoughts, problems and worries were forgotten as this was the realm of God.

Soon after daybreak Gangu knocked at the door and brought in a tray of food, "I trust you slept well. I have brought you some breakfast."

"Thank you Gangu."

"I also enquired about the Guru. Everyone in the village is talking about what happened and how the Mughals double-crossed him when he came out of the fort."

"Is there any news of where the Guru is now?"

"No Mata Gujri, I heard after they crossed the river they headed towards the town of Chamkaur, but that's all I know."

"Is there any other news?"

"Well, um...er... I wasn't going to mention it, but the Governor has offered a huge reward for the capture of any of your family."

Mata Gujri looked Gangu straight in the eye, Gangu looked away and nervously started moving the cups and plates off the tray onto the table.

"Gangu, where is my bag?"

"Wasn't it here on the table last night?"

"Yes it was, so where is it now?"

"How should I know? You're getting quite old Mata Gujri and probably forgot where you put it?"

"No Gangu, it has definitely been stolen."

"STOLEN! O MY GOD - A THIEF IN MY OWN HOUSE!"

Gangu ran outside and started shouting to the neighbours, "I'VE HAD A BREAK IN!"

After sometime the commotion died down and he came back inside.

"I've reported it to the police Mata Gujri, I'm sure they will capture the thief."

"Gangu my son, we can't hide our mistakes from God. Is there anything you want to tell me?"

"I don't know what you mean Mata Gujri."

"You thought I was sleeping when you sneaked into the room last night, but I was meditating and was aware of everything."

"HOW DARE YOU ACCUSE ME."

"Now calm down Gangu. I don't care for the bag of gold. I am an old woman, what need do I have for gold. I care about your soul. Ask God for forgiveness - you can't hide your actions from God, Gangu."

"I AM RISKING MY LIFE BY HIDING YOU HERE AND THIS IS HOW YOU ACCUSE ME."

"Gangu stealing is bad, stealing the Guru's gold coins is even worse. You imagine that happiness will come to you by having the gold, but you have eaten poison. For your own sake give it back - it's not too late my son. God forgives."

"YOU MAKE ME SICK! I thought you were worth helping, but you Sikhs are all the same. I don't need friends like you - in fact I am going to tell the Governor where you are."

"Gangu if you turn us in it is because you are not satisfied with gold you already have stolen, but want the reward too. Gangu, you promised you would take us to Guru Gobind Singh. And I promise you the Guru will forgive you and give you ten times the gold as a reward."

Gangu was silent for a second while he thought about how rich he would be, "Why should I trust you? For all I know Guru Gobind Singh is dead."

Gangu stormed out of the house and returned with a few local police officers. They arrested Mata Gujri and the young princes. As they marched them out, a small crowd gathered. Mata Gujri looked at Gangu in the eye, "What have you done my son, what have you done?"

Gangu turned his back and counted the gold coins from his reward.

After being locked up in the local police station they were taken to face trial at the Governor's court in the town of Sirhind.

They were locked up at the top of a tall tower. There was a cold stone floor to sit on and windowless holes in the walls. An icy wind kept them company that night.

Mata Gujri sat the young princes beside her and wrapped her thick shawl around them, like a mother bird taking her young chicks under her warm wings.

Huddled together and shivering, Mata Gujri sang the Guru's verses about Indestructible Waheguru. The young princes joined her and soon they forgot about the cold, dark cell.

Suddenly, the heavy wooden door creaked open. A guard stepped forward and slid a plate of food towards them. As he left he said, "You will be taken to court in the morning. Governor Wazir Khan himself will hear your case."

Mata Gujri pushed away the tray, the guard screwed his face up and marched out. She hugged the young princes closer and said, "Don't be afraid my children."

"We're not afraid of anyone but God. We may be locked up but our spirits are always free," said Baba Zorawar Singh.

Baba Fateh Singh lifted his head from Mata Gujri's lap and looked at her with his soft brown eyes, "Tell us about the time when grandfather was locked up."

Mata Gujri took a deep breath and held back her emotions. "Your grandfather was a peaceful man. When the leaders of the Hindu nation came to him he was deeply saddened to hear their story."

"That's when they were being forced to convert to Islam or being killed."

"That's right Zorawar Singh, then your grandfather went to Delhi to protest against the Emperor."

"They locked him up in that animal cage didn't they?"

"They locked him up and tortured his closest Sikhs in front of his eyes. But the Sikhs died like heroes refusing to convert to Islam."

Mata Gujri sat up straight and spoke with defiance, "The Emperor then gave your grandfather three choices."

"Grandma, they told him if he did a miracle it would prove he was a holy man and he would be free to go. Or he would have to convert to Islam. Otherwise they would kill him like they killed his Sikhs."

"That's right Zorawar Singh."

Zorawar Singh threw off the shawl and jumped up. "Fateh Singh, our grandfather told the Emperor that he was not a cheap magician. He didn't come to entertain him with miracles."

"The Emperor must have been really cross," said Fateh Singh.

"Then our grandfather said it was not right to force someone to change their religion."

Fateh Singh looked up at his brother and said, "The Emperor must have got really angry when he heard that."

"Yes brother, that's when the Emperor ordered the prophet of peace Guru Tegh Bahadur to be beheaded."

"Children, your grandfather didn't follow the path of Hinduism. But, he did believe that everyone had the rights to their beliefs. He was so saddened that the Emperor had abused the human rights of the innocent Hindus. He gave his life to protect their right to be free."

Zorawar Singh added, "He smashed his body, like a vase, on the Emperor of Delhi's head."

"Grandma..."

"Yes, Fateh Singh."

"Grandma, pray for us so that we too will be fearless tomorrow when the Governor questions us."

All three stood up with pressed palms and tilted heads humbly requesting Waheguru's to make them fearless.

They were taken to court for the next three days.

On the third day the Governor was about to pass sentence. He asked them one last time, "Will you convert to Islam?"

"Our grandfather gave up his life but not his faith. So shall we!" replied the defiant Zorawar Singh.

"What would you do if I released you?"

"We will go and rejoin the Khalsa Army. Then we will come here and destroy you," replied the courageous Fateh Singh.

The Governor was furious, "In that case I sentence you to death."

One of the Governor's advisors jumped up, "Your excellency, they are only children. It is against Islam to harm women or children."

"They will only grow up to be like their father Gobind Singh. I will give them one last chance - build a brick wall around them and after each layer is completed ask them if they will convert. If they do they are free to go. If they don't ..."

The young princes stood side by side as the brick wall was built around them. Each time they were asked to convert they refused and shouted slogans of victory to God.

When the final layer of bricks was level with their shoulders, Zorawar Singh looked down to Fateh Singh, "I will always be by your side brother."

The executioner's sword swung swiftly and took Fateh Singh's head clean off. Another mighty swing saw Zorawar Singh's head land next to his brother.

Mata Gujri was meditating in the cold dark tower and new instantly her young princes had left this world. A soldier came in to give her the news. But, she had already closed her eyes and prayed to Waheguru for freedom. Her soul bird flew with the young princes to the God's Realm of Truth. Forever at peace, forever together.

Back in Gangu's village, the local police decided to find Mata Gujri's stolen bag for themselves. They went to Gangu's house and tortured him slowly to death trying to get him to reveal where he had hidden the gold coins.

When Guru Gobind Singh heard of the death of his mother and children at the hands of Governor Wazir Khan, he plucked a weed from under his feet and said, "The tyrant has been uprooted, Sirhind will be destroyed."

Six years later in 1710, the Khalsa Army under Banda Singh Bahadur upheld the Guru's words and Governor Wazir Khan was killed in battle. They also destroyed the whole of Sirhind except for the house of the Governor's advisor as he was the only one in the whole town who had stood up for the young princes.

UNITE WITH GOD

Countless sparks rise from one fire

then merge in the fire again.

Countless particles rise from the dust

then blend with the dust again.

Countless waves form on the sea

then fall and merge with the ocean again.

In the same way,

everything springs from God

and unites with God again.

Guru Gobind Singh

*In memory of where Mata Gujri, Baba Zorawar Singh
and Baba Fateh Singh were locked up, stands Gurdwara
Tanda Buraj - the Cold Tower. Sirhind, Punjab.*

Gurdwara Fatehgarh Sahib has been built around the original brick wall used in the execution of Baba Zorawar Singh and Baba Fateh Singh. Sirhind, Punjab.

THE
FEARLESS
LEADER

Mai Bhago The Teenager

Set around 1695, about ten years before "The Siege"
Jhabbal village, Amritsar, Punjab.

"Why are you crying cousin Sursutty?"

"Bhago, I can't help it. I've just read about how the Mughal Emperor beheaded Guru Tegh Bahadur twenty years ago. It makes me feel empty inside and I feel afraid of going anywhere in case I am attacked by the Mughals."

"That's not what Guru Tegh Bahadur would have wanted Sursutty. You have to be strong. Remember our Guru told us not to be frightened of anything nor should we frighten anyone."

"I know Bhago, but what can we do against someone as powerful as the Emperor? We are just village girls. We'll get married, cook and clean and worry about if our husbands and sons will survive against Mughal oppression."

"Sursutty, the Emperor is not powerful, he is nobody. We have the true Emperor on our side. Guru Gobind Singh is the true king and I am going to fight by his side. I'm not going to just sit here and watch innocent people being killed." Sursutty stopped crying and looked up at the teenage Bhago – she was not like any other girl in the village. She had so much spirit.

"Sursutty, do you want to see something?" Bhago unravelled the cloth bundle under her arm. She pulled out a small sword from its scabbard. It shone under the midday sun and was beautifully polished.

"Wow – where did you get that from?"

"It's my brothers. Do you want to come and practice with me. I cut down two thick banana tree branches in one swoop yesterday."

A middle-aged woman came out of the house towards the girls sitting on the grass by the dirt-track.

"Bhago – are you talking about fighting again? I'm ashamed to call you my daughter. Get inside and help me cook the food. Your father and brother will be back from the fields soon."

78

Bhago quickly wrapped the sword up and whispered to Sursutty. "Meet me here before sunset – while there's still some light. I'm going to sneak out with my brother's spear."

Later that night as the family dined, Bhago's father turned to her mother. "A friend of mine told me of a good match for Bhago. They're from Patti village – not too far from here."

They talked about Bhago like she wasn't there.

"It's about time she got married – all she does nowadays is sneak out with the weapons."

"Sister, is that true?"

Bhago did not say anything and carried on clearing away the dishes.

"You know those weapons are for our defence. We could get attacked at any time. I can't believe you would put our lives at risk by sneaking out with them. What would happen if you lost them?"

"Tell me brother, what good are the weapons

when the men are in the fields and we are home alone. You should teach me how to use them so I can defend the village."

Her father interrupted, "Bhago you're just a girl – you should scream and we'll come running."

"Why should I scream. I am not afraid anyone. I'll send those Mughals screaming if they come near me!"

"Mother, I think you are right, it's time we got my sister married while she still listens to us."

"I don't want to get married. I want to go and fight with Guru Gobind Singh and get justice for what the Mughals did to Guru Tegh Bahadur."

"Listen Bhago, I'm your father and you'll do what I say. I've found a good family for you. They own a lot of land and are very respectable. That's it. Our Guru's told us to get married – so stop dreaming about running away to join the army. That's a man's job."

Bhago went to her bedroom and sat staring at the

reddening sky. She calmed herself down with her evening meditation, and prayed to Guru Gobind Singh to grant her wish of joining his soldiers.

Just then there was a knock on the door. Her brother walked in with his prized spear in his hand. "So you want to learn to fight! Come on then!"

Bhago jumped up and hugged him with a huge smile on her face. They went outside. Bhago looked around for Sursutty, but she was nowhere to be seen. She was not destined for greatness.

***

Mai Bhago The Wife

Around 1700. Patti village, Amritsar, Punjab.

"One of the cows gave birth this morning. To twins! God has blessed us Bhago."

"That's the best news we've had since I married you Nidhan!"

"I have more great news too. There's going to be

a huge warrior festival at Anandpur in a few days. Guru Gobind Singh has sent letters to all the villages requesting everyone to come."

"That is great news, I've dying to have the sacred vision of Guru Gobind Singh."

Next morning Nidhan and Bhago joined five hundred Sikh men and forty women. The impressive group travelled for a couple of days through the heat of the Spring months. As they came out from the hilly forests their senses filled with awe and wonder.

Hundreds of tents could be seen all around. Warrior Sikhs walked about wearing blue uniforms strapped with battle-axes and swords. A huge line of Sikh drummers were seen practising. They beat out the rhythm of horses charging into battle. Others practised their fighting skills infront of huge crowds. Bhago's group found a clear field and settled down. Nidhan rode into the crowds for some time then returned.

"Bhago, there's a great programme tomorrow. We'll get up early and go and listen to the morning prayer. Then all day long crowds of people are going to join the Khalsa by getting initiated. Finally, to top it all there will be a huge procession to celebrate. It's going to be amazing."

"Nidhan, this is the moment I have been waiting for since my childhood. Tomorrow we get to join the Khalsa - the Army of God. We will be able to fight by our Guru's side."

After the initiation ceremony, everyone came out with love in their hearts. They felt spiritual peace. Guru Gobind Singh told them they were all brothers and sisters, and that they were all equal. Mai Bhago became a princess, her new name was Bhag Kaur. Her husband become a lion – Nidhan Singh.

A profound change came over Bhag Kaur. She wanted to stay with the saint warriors of the Khalsa. God's name had penetrated her heart. The years of training with weapons at home would be put to good use here. Nidhan Singh too felt the call of the Khalsa, but he said to his wife, "We have to go back home. Who will look after our farm and animals? We have a duty to them as well."

Four years passed and both Nidhan Singh's and Bhag Kaur's spirituality increased day by day. Waheguru was preparing them for a great sacrifice. One day a letter came from Guru Gobind Singh to all the villages. Once again he requested the initiated Sikh men to join him at Anandpur, but this time they were warned that many of them would not return to their wives and children.

The times had gradually worsened. Many neighbouring Hindu Warlords saw the Guru and his Khalsa army as a threat. To make things worse, Emperor Aurangzeb was intent on destroying anyone who did not convert to Islam. Aurangzeb had already imposed extra taxes on non-Muslims and dismissed all Hindus from Government jobs. The Khalsa were involved in many battles. Guru Gobind Singh needed reinforcements, but he only requested the men first.

Having read the letter from the Guru requesting soldiers, five hundred brave Sikhs, including Nidhan Singh, left for Anandpur. On the way, they were attacked by an army of Mughal soldiers. A long battle ensued into the night, but eventually the Sikhs won. However the price they paid was very high, half of them had been martyred. The rest of them reached Anandpur and received a hero's welcome.

Soon after, the Mughal siege of Anandgarh Fort started. The Khalsa spent the hot summer and cold winter by Guru Gobind Singh's side slowly starving to death.

When the Mughals offered the Sikhs safe passage from the Fort, Guru Gobind Singh saw it as a trick. But it had all became too much for some Sikhs.

Forty of the warrior Sikhs from the villages in Bhag Kaur's area approached the Guru. They said, "We wish to take up the offer of safe passage. We want to leave."

The Guru told them they would be disobeying him if they went. But they were so adamant that the Guru said to them, "If you want to leave, then you have to put it into writing. Sign this desertion letter that says you are not my Sikhs any more."

With heads bowed low, Nidhan Singh and his group signed the desertion letter and packed their belongings.

The Guru's mother and close Sikhs suggested to the Guru perhaps they could trust the Mughals. But the Guru said he would prove it was a trick. Guru Gobind Singh sent out mules loaded with old sacks full of rubbish and rags. The Mughals thought the Sikhs were taking up the offer of safe passage, and true to form they came charging and attacked the mules.

In the confusion the forty deserters escaped in small groups under the cover of darkness.

By the time the forty deserters reached their home villages a great deal had happened to Guru Gobind Singh. His entire family and closest Sikhs had later left the fort only to have been attacked with tragic consequences.

When Guru Gobind Singh was reunited with his wife Sundri and Mother of the Khalsa Mata Sahib Kaur. They asked where the young princes were? Guru Gobind Singh pointed to his Khalsa followers, "For these thousands I sacrificed the other four. So long as these sons of mine are alive, I will not consider the death of my four sons to have been for nothing."

Over the coming months the Guru sought justice. On the face of it he had almost lost everything - his father, mother, four sons and bravest Sikhs. But far from being depressed, Guru Gobind Singh wrote two letters of victory to Emperor Aurangzeb telling him :

What if you killed my four sons?
When I like a coiled snake remain behind.
What type of bravery was that?
By extinguishing the sparks
you have flamed the fire!

ZafarNama

As the days passed by the Guru rebuilt his Khalsa Army. Guru Gobind Singh was once again being hunted by Governor Wazir Khan's army. When Bhag Kaur heard the news her fighting spirit took over.

***

Bhag Kaur The Warrior Leader

Late December, 1705. The village meeting area.

"It seems like yesterday when the older sons of Guru Gobind Singh were killed in the Battle of Chamkaur. We were all shocked by this, but there was nothing we could do at that time."

Wearing the Khalsa uniform and strapped with weapons she stood on an outdoor stage. Bhag Kaur looked out across the sea of villagers.

"A few days later the Governor killed Guru Gobind Singh's younger sons in Sirhind. Once again we were shocked, but we stood here unable to do anything about it."

The memory was still fresh and the women wiped away tears as they listened.

"Do not be sad brothers and sisters. We are not helpless any longer. The time has come for us to fight. Our Guru is nearby and needs brave warriors. An army of ten thousand is after him. We will be outnumbered, we may not come back alive, but we will fight back until we have destroyed every last Mughal from our land. EVERY LAST MUGHAL."

A huge battle cry was issued from the crowd, "BOLAY SO NIHAL... SAT SREE AKAL!"

A couple of women in the crowd looked at each other, the older lady spoke, "Can you see the light of God around her. She is a radiant saint."

The younger lady replied, "She's amazing. Since the news came that the Guru's sons had been murdered, she has not cried, she has not wailed or questioned God like the other women. She has just been one hundred percent focused on meditation and war."

Bhag Kaur's powerful voice interrupted the women.

"Brothers and sisters, before we can go to war, we have to deal with the ones who have brought us shame."

The forty deserters from the siege at Anandgarh Fort became nervous. Nidhan Singh was one of them. The older lady turned and looked at him, "Your wife is a brave woman - she would never have left the Guru like you did."

Nidhan Singh took a deep sigh and looked to his wife for inspiration.

"We have forty deserters standing amongst us who saved themselves, but in doing so let the four sons of the Guru die. We have forty standing amongst us who decided to disobey their Guru and leave him in his hour of need. Well let me tell those forty this: you deserted your Guru to save your body. But sooner or later, your precious body will desert you. Who will save you then? There will be no Guru to take your soul! Without the Guru's protection you will be smashed to pieces like a small boat ripped apart by a furious storm."

Another huge battle cry was issued from the crowd, "BOLAY SO NIHAL ... SAT SREE AKAL!"

"Let me say one thing to those forty deserters. If they wont go back and fight then the women will go instead. Give us your weapons and we'll give you our bangles. Dressed in your uniforms we will go and fight for the Guru and sacrifice our lives for him. With our blood we will wash away the shame you have brought on all the Sikhs of this area."

Mahan Singh stepped towards the stage representing the forty. He pressed his palms together and humbly looked to the ground as he spoke.

"Bhag Kaur, since leaving our Guru we can't sleep or eat. Everyday we feel a knife stabbing us in the heart. We are burning in our guilt. Only Guru Gobind Singh can put it out with the water of forgiveness. But, how can we show our faces to him after everything that has happened?"

"Mahan Singh, you made a grave mistake, but it is not too late to make up for it. Gather your forty Sikhs, we will leave early tomorrow to meet the Guru."

Bhag Kaur looked up at the huge crowd, "Who will go with us to fight for the Guru?"

Deafening voices shouted in readiness, "BOLAY
SO NIHAL... SAT SREE AKAL!"

***

Bhag Kaur At The Battle Of Mukhtsar

Mahan Singh and Bhag Kaur rode like the wind
leading their band of Khalsa warriors. As they
passed through villages, many more Sikhs joined
them.

They finally caught up with Guru Gobind Singh
when suddenly the Guru's watchman in the treetop
shouted, "Guru! Guru! Thousands of Mughals
are heading this way."

Mahan Singh addressed his group. "Our Guru
needs us, we disowned him once and have lived a
shameful life. Let us regain our honour and fight
with the Khalsa."

He turned to the Guru, "We will lure the Mughals
here to the lower ground."

The Guru added, "The rest of us will go uphill

with the archers."

Guru Gobind Singh rode uphill with most of the Khalsa army. In the meantime Bhag Kaur's Sikhs spread big, white sheets on the shrubs. This would trick the Mughals into thinking that thousands of Sikhs were camped here. They would then come and attack them on the lower ground.

Fearlessly, the small group of Sikhs hid waiting to take the huge army by surprise.

As they approached, Guru Gobind Singh ordered his soldiers to fire arrows down hill. This took the Mughals by surprise. Then they were bombarded with bullets. Bhag Kaur was seen fighting on the front line. She accurately fired her rifle like a true soldier.

The Mughal army rushed forward again and again but had to retreat every time the fierce volley of bullets and arrows. Once the bullets and arrows were used up, the Sikhs charged forward in small batches and fought the Mughals in hand-to-hand combat.

When Bhag Kaur's turn came she raced ahead with a long spear. She killed a soldier and created panic amongst the Mughals. Eventually she was struck by a mighty blow and collapsed onto the ground with wounds all over her body.

So many Mughal soldiers had been killed that the Governor's army had no choice left but to retreat. Guru Gobind Singh rode back to the battlefield to claim victory. He found heaps of heads and body parts scattered everywhere. Blood-soaked Khalsa soldiers were all around him. Slowly and carefully, the Guru knelt by each dead soldier and bestowed his blessings :

Here is my Khalsa.
He commands twenty thousand,
He commands thirty thousand.
He rules the hearts of a hundred thousand.
He takes so many steps towards me
and is blessed with happiness accordingly.

Suraj Prakash

When Guru Gobind Singh lifted Mahan Singh's head gently and hugged him like father and son.

He saw he still had a few breaths left, "Mahan Singh open your eyes. Words cannot express how pleased I am with you."

"Guru Gobind Singh we made a terrible mistake when we deserted you. We feared death, but now it is my turn to die I feel no fear. I only feel your love my Guru."

"Mahan Singh your soul is truly free, truly liberated. Do you have a last request? Ask for anything Mahan Singh, I will move heaven and earth for a true Khalsa like you."

"Tear up the desertion letter and free our souls from the shame."

Guru Gobind Singh reached inside his uniform and pulled out the signed desertion letter. He tore it up and threw it to the wind. Bhai Mahan Singh closed his eyes and breathed his last on the Guru's lap.

The Guru then kneeled beside Bhag Kaur and realised she too was alive. She opened her eyes and saw the Guru's face in all his radiance. It lifted her spirits to the highest realm.

Guru Gobind Singh looked up and signalled to some Singhs to bring treatment for her wounds. Bhag Kaur mustered up every last bit of energy and spoke, "My Guru, once I went with my husband to Anandpur. We wanted your holy vision and to be blessed with brave sons who would grow up and join the Khalsa. But you had left Anandpur."

"These are troubled times my daughter. I never stay in one place for too long."

"When I heard your sons had been killed, I lost all hopes of raising children. I vowed I would come and fight alongside you one day."

She asked what had happened to the forty deserters including her husband Nidhan Singh. Guru Gobind Singh told her, "They are no longer deserters dear child, they are the forty liberated ones. Your husband died a hero's death on the battlefield."

Later on Guru Gobind Singh gathered fire wood

and cremated their bodies. He said, "The place where a saint dies is considered to be holy. The forty martyrs have laid down their lives after giving up worldly desires. They have achieved salvation (mukhti). This place will be known as Mukhtsar."

Bhag Kaur dedicated the rest of her life to the Khalsa and dressed in a Khalsa warrior's uniform, she served Guru Gobind Singh as one of his ten personal guards.

After Aurangzeb read the Guru's letters of victory he lost his confidence. He had been a powerful Emperor, but now in his nineties, death was on his mind all of the time.

When he read the Guru's letter he feared for his soul. The Guru's words struck him like an arrow in his heart :

If one million soldiers attack one person,
then God protects that one person.
Your eyes are set on your army and wealth,
but my eyes are fixed only on God.

*You are proud of your riches
and the countries you have conquered,
but I have God's support behind me.*

*Do not be careless in this transitory world,
This world is changing everywhere.*

ZafarNama

Emperor Aurangzeb died a few years later in 1707. He wrote in his will, "There is no doubt that I have been the Emperor of India and I have ruled over this country. But, I am sorry to say that during my lifetime, I had not been able to do any good deed. My inner soul is cursing me as a sinner. But now it is too late . . . God should not make anyone an Emperor. In my opinion the Emperor is the most unfortunate person in the world."

Guru Gobind Singh continued to try and get justice peacefully from the new Emperor Bahadur Shah. The Guru told the Emperor how the Governor of Sirhind, Wazir Khan had been committing crimes against the people. The Guru said he wanted the Governor to be brought to justice for all the crimes including killing his younger sons. The Guru waited over a year for the Emperor to decide whether to prosecute and followed him to South India.

Governor Wazir Khan was extremely worried he would get punished, so he sent an assassin to kill the Guru. He infiltrated the Sikhs and stabbed the sleeping Guru in the chest. With lightning fast reflexes, the Guru drew his sword and chopped off the assassin's head. The great Guru fully recovered, but soon afterwards he told the Sikhs that his time had come to leave them.

Before he left his earthly body, the Guru had appointed Banda Singh Bahadur to ride back to Punjab and organise the Sikhs. One of the first things he and the Khalsa army did was to destroy Governor Wazir Khan in battle a few years later.

Guru Gobind Singh had taught them that when all peaceful means for justice had been exhausted, then it was right to draw the sword.

***

Bhag Kaur The Wise Old Lioness

Guru Gobind Singh left his earthly body in 1708 in Nanded, South India. Bhag Kaur left that place and settled nearby in the village Jinvara. She spent the rest of her life absorbed in meditation and selfless service.

Even as a wise, old lioness, Bhag Kaur was fearless. Once she passed through a mainly Hindu village and heard a woman screaming. She ran down the street and around the corner. To her horror there was roaring fire and a woman being dragged towards it by a group of men.

Bhag Kaur dashed forward and rescued the lady. Just seeing Bhag Kaur in her Khalsa uniform was enough to stop the men attacking her. They started shouting at Bhag Kaur, "How dare you insult our beliefs. That women is not pure. Her punishment is to be burnt alive."

Bhag Kaur was furious and marched away. She took the woman in and asked her what had happened.

"My name is Ratni, my husband died not so long ago – so I am all alone. A lot of the elders believe that I should have committed *Sati* by jumping into the fire at my husband's cremation, but I didn't. So now they turn away from me as I walk down the street. Then yesterday a young Muslim man started flirting with me, he grabbed my hand and I screamed. The villagers saw what was happening, but no one helped me."

Ratni started crying. Bhag Kaur comforted her and asked, "So didn't they punish the man?"

"No, they decided it was my fault, that I was impure and should be burnt alive. That's when you rescued me."

Ratni fell to Bhag Kaur's feet, "You are my mother, you are the only one that cares about me."

"Ratni, the Guru cares about everyone of God's children. Join the Guru's family like I have and the Guru will be your spiritual Father, and Mata Sahib Kaur will be your spiritual mother. We are sisters, we are equal, there is no need to touch my feet. Now get up."

Bhag Kaur lifted Ratni and hugged her. Sometime later, Ratni too dedicated her life to the Guru's way by receiving the holy Amrit.

Bhag Kaur lived a long life. In her memory her meditation hut has become Gurdwara Tap Asthan Mai Bhago, and there is a small room with her long single barrel rifle and other belongings at Hazoor Sahib, Nanded.

Also in her memory the Gurdwara Mata Bhag Kaur stands at the place where she lay wounded after the battle of Mukhtsar.

Bhag Kaur lived up to the prayer of Guru Gobind Singh :

MAY I DIE FIGHTING

Give me this gift Lord,

that I never refrain from righteous deeds.

That I have no fear when fighting the enemy,

That I attain victory with faith and fortitude,

That I keep your teachings close to my mind.

Lord, my desire is that I sing your praises

and when the end of this life draws near,

may I die fighting,

with limitless courage in the battlefield.

Guru Gobind Singh

Gurdwara Mukhtsar.   The forty martyrs died fighting
here and were cremated by Guru Gobind Singh.

Gurdwara Mata Bagh Kaur marks the spot where she lay wounded in the Battle of Mukhtsar. Punjab.

ACKNOWLEDGMENTS

Great appreciation goes to Harjit Singh "Artist" for the wonderful artwork and Taranjit Singh for all the professional design work and the original website.

I would also like to thank Baldev Singh for the translations from "Ardashak Singhnia" by Karam Singh (published by Niranjan Singh & Sons, Amritsar, 1981).

I also referenced the Punjabi book "Mai Bhago" by Principal Nihal Singh Russ (published by Chattar Singh Jiwan Singh, Amritsar 1996). Historical dates were based on the book "Guru Gobind Singh and Khalsa Discipline" by Dalip Singh. I also read "A History Of The Sikh People" by Dr Gopal Singh.

The Guru's words in "The Cremation" story are a direct translation from the victory letters. Artitstic license has been used in all the stories to create dialogues and situations to bring them more detail, but the spirit of this amazing story has not been changed.

Finally I would like to thank Manbir and Pavan Kaur for reviewing the draft versions.

GLOSSARY

Amrit

Holy water prepared in an iron bowl and stirred by the double-edged sword in the Sikh initiation ceremony.

Bolay So Nihal, Sat Sree Akal

Sikh battle-cry. Meaning "Whoever speaks it will be Joyous : God Is True"

Emperor Aurangzeb

One of the last Emperors of the Mughal Dynasty. He reigned from 1658 to 1707. He promoted aggressive conversions to Islam.

Guru

Spiritual Enlightener.

Guru Gobind Singh Jee

Tenth Master of the Sikhs. Destroyed tyrants defended saints.

Khalsa

1.An initiated Sikh,

2. The Sikh Army created in 1699

Mughal

The Mughal Dynasty was a line of Muslim emperors who reigned India from 1526 to 1858.

Waheguru

God - 'The Wonderful Being who takes us from Darkness to Light'.

Waheguru Jee Ka Khalsa,
Waheguru Jee Kee Fateh

Sikh Greeting

Harjit Singh

I have been blessed with serving the Guru's holy congregation. I began writing to express my emotions, and when the love affair with God started - the pen moved like the wind. I am married to Davinder Kaur and we have two daughters, HarSimran and Tavleen. When I see them, I know Waheguru has given me a mission to make many inspiring books for the next generation.

Website : www.Sikh-Heroes.com
Email : Harjit@sikh-heroes.com

THE
WARRIOR
PRINCESS

WWW.SIKH-HEROES.COM

THE WARRIOR PRINCESS 1

BY
HARJIT SINGH